Karate is a game— and an art

This book will show you the ways in which you can make a karate chop or any other karate punch. It will also show you how to defend yourself against your opponent's blows. Then you will have reached the point where there is no reason to hit your opponent. You know you can beat him if you have to, and therefore you can afford to be polite to him. This book's purpose is to develop good sportsmanship and respect for others. . . .

JUNIOR KARATE

RUSSELL KOZUKI

Chief Instructor,
International Schools
of Self-Defense

Photographs by the author

AN ARCHWAY PAPERBACK
Published by POCKET BOOKS • NEW YORK

The author and publishers wish to thank the following boys for posing as models in this book: Dennis Cheng, Robert Cirna, Danny Lam, and Sonny Ng.

An Archway Paperback published by
POCKET BOOKS, a division of Simon & Schuster, Inc.
1230 Avenue of the Americas, New York, N.Y. 10020

Copyright © 1971 by Sterling Publishing Co., Inc.
Cover photograph copyright © 1986 A. Boccaccio/The Image Bank

Published by arrangement with Sterling Publishing Co., Inc.
Library of Congress Catalog Card Number: 71-167665

ISBN: 0-671-62489-X

First Pocket Books printing November, 1977

17   16   15   14   13   12

AN ARCHWAY PAPERBACK and colophon are registered trademarks of Simon & Schuster, Inc.

Printed in the U.S.A.

IL 4+

Contents

JUNIOR KARATE

Before You Begin

KARATE IS a sport—a game. When you practice karate or enter a karate contest, you do not actually strike your opponent's head or hit any part of his body hard. If you punched him, you would hurt him, so you block his blows and he blocks yours. The idea is to show that you could break through his defense and hit him if you really wanted to. Your opponent tries to prove he can defend himself by blocking your blows.

This book will show you the ways in which you can make a karate chop or any other karate punch. It will also show you how to defend yourself against your opponent's blows. Then you will have reached the point where there is no reason to hit your opponent. You know you can beat him, if you have to, and therefore you can afford to be polite to him. This book's purpose is to develop good sportsmanship and respect for others.

1

Real fights occur because one boy thinks he can beat another but the second boy does not believe it. So they enter into a contest. If the contest is a karate contest and it is conducted as a game it will prove who is right without either boy being hurt.

All of the exercises *(katas)* in this book are harmless. Never strike your opponent's head, whether with your hand or your foot. Always stop before you make contact. Block all of his blows with your arms and hands.

Exercises

As IN other sports, you should "warm up" before beginning karate. There is far less chance of strain or injury when your muscles and your joints have been loosened up. Also the exercises in themselves are first-rate body conditioners. Here are some typical karate exercises.

Neck Exercise

Illus. 1—Stand with hands on hips. Rotate your head from right to left slowly in a wide, circular motion. Repeat this several times. Now rotate your head left to right in the same manner. This exercise relaxes your neck muscles and relieves tension.

Illus. 1

Push-Ups

Illus. 2—Push-ups are very good for general body conditioning. Do push-ups on the first two knuckles of your fist to strengthen your wrist. Push-ups can also be done on fingertips to make your fingers stronger. Work slowly and keep your back straight.

Illus. 2

Illus. 3   Illus. 4

Shoulder Exercise

Illus. 3 and 4—Cross your arms overhead. Keep arms straight and stiff. Now move arms downward to your sides. Press arms backwards to put pressure on your shoulder and chest muscles.

Illus. 5

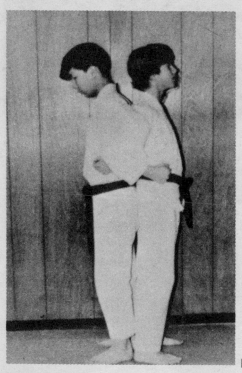

Illus. 6

Illus. 7

Leg-Stretching Exercise

Illus. 5—Sit on the floor with your legs as wide apart as possible. Lean your upper body forward and grasp your ankle or foot with both hands. Repeat several times and do the same on the other leg. This exercise is also good for the waist.

Two-Man Exercise

Illus. 6 and 7—Stand back to back with your partner, with arms locked tightly. Now bend forward slowly, carrying your partner on your back. Straighten up, and let your partner lift you in the same manner. Avoid sudden moves.

7

Balance and Stance

You know that when you balance a pencil on your finger, the balance point is very close to the center of the pencil. Have you ever thought of at what point your body is balanced? Those who started karate (many years ago on the island of Okinawa) believed that the body's balance point is located in the area just below your navel. They call it the *hara*. In karate, it is good to keep your body low so that the midpoint or *hara* is close to the ground. You cannot then be pushed off balance so easily because your center of gravity is low.

Merely bending low is not enough. You must train your mind to think always of your *hara* and push forward the area around your navel. When exhaling, press downward as much as you can and you will see that this brings your diaphragm, or your breathing apparatus, very low to the ground. Correct breathing and keeping your mind on the *hara* will make it easier for you to keep your body balance strong.

Many different stances are used in karate, each with strong and weak points. The ones that you will find most useful at the beginning are the natural or ready stance, the forward stance, and the back stance. In all three, the body balance is kept low.

The Natural or Ready Stance

Illus. 8—From this natural, upright position, you are "ready" to move in any direction and into any other stance. Your feet should be about as far apart as your shoulders, with your fists at your sides and a little to the front of your body. Bow from the natural, or ready, stance as a kind of salute and a sign of respect for your opponent.

Illus. 8

Forward Stance

Illus. 9 and 10—About 60 per cent of your body weight is on your front foot in this stance. Your forward leg must be kept straight up and down. If your body weight is too far forward, it will be hard to move quickly. Hold your rear leg straight and tense with your heel flat on the ground if you can. The toes of your rear foot should be turned towards the front at about a 45-degree angle. Keep your back straight and head up.

Illus. 9

Illus. 10

Illus. 11

Stepping Forward

Illus. 12

How to Move in the Forward Stance

Illus. 11—To move forward, bring your rear foot up alongside and past your front leg by sliding it barely above the ground. When your rear foot ends its forward slide, tense and straighten your back leg. Keep both heels flat. The basic rule in body shifting or movement is always to move your hips first and your legs afterwards.

To move back from the forward stance, bend your rear knee and slide your front foot to the rear.

Back Stance

Illus. 13—More flexible than the forward stance, the back stance is mainly used for defense. Many karate fighters prefer this stance because it is easy for them to shift into another stance whenever the need arises. About 70 per cent of your body weight is kept on your back leg. You lock your hips at a 45-degree angle, with your body in the half-front facing position.

How to Move in the Back Stance

Illus. 14, 15 and 16—To move forward, bring your rear leg up and next to your front leg. Remember to move your hips first. Do not pick up your foot. Instead, glide forward, and shift your body weight to your front leg, as your rear leg moves to the front.

Illus. 13

Illus. 14

Illus. 15

Illus. 16

Illus. 17

The Horse Stance

Illus. 17 is so called because it resembles the position of a man on horseback. Your feet are placed about twice as far apart as your shoulders, with your legs tensed and your back straight. Bend both knees and push outward to the sides. This is a very strong defensive stance, since only one side of your body is exposed to an opponent's attack.

16

How to Move in the Horse Stance

Illus. 18 and 19—To move to the left from the horse stance, bring your right leg in front of

Illus. 18

Illus. 19

your left. Stay low and keep your back straight.
(Illus. 20). Then move your left foot two shoulder widths apart in the same direction.

Illus. 20

PIVOTING OR STEP TURNING

Sometimes it is necessary to turn quickly in the opposite direction to protect yourself from a sudden attack from the rear. To do this from the *back stance*, pivot on the balls of both feet and adjust your body weight in the opposite direction at the same time.

Pivoting to the rear from the *forward stance* (Illus. 21 and 22) requires moving your back

Illus. 21

Illus. 22

foot straight across about 10 inches past the heel of your forward foot while keeping your back straight and your body low. Turn now on the balls of both feet to your rear. At the same time shift the weight of your body forward. About 60 per cent of your body weight is now on your front foot and 40 per cent on your rear leg, which is stiff and tensed.

Power

TO GET more power while using speed at the same time, you must center or focus your attention on your muscles. For example, a strong, but slow, pushing type of punch is not half as powerful as the same punch thrown with blinding speed!

To get power into your punch, your muscles must be tight and tensed. However, this will cut down your speed if your muscles stay tense during the time you are throwing the punch. On the other hand, if you keep your muscles loose, your punch will be much faster but weak.

The trick is to throw the punch loose and tense your muscles just before your punch hits the target! Then you must relax your muscles immediately so that you can move quickly to your next technique.

Exhale your breath the very same instant you

tense your muscles! This is called "focus" in karate. A well-trained *karateka* (karate athlete) can focus a powerful punch an inch from his opponent's face without hurting him! He can strike like a coiled snake. Speed and co-ordination are what make the focus of power possible.

This basic principle applies also to punching, kicking, or blocking techniques. But, just understanding the basic karate principles is not enough! To make them work, much hard training is required. You must work until the techniques become a part of you. Then you will be able to make the right move quickly without thinking! The amazing speed and power of the trained *karateka* can be developed only through hard work and serious training. There are no easy roads, no short-cuts, no secret methods to karate power! The really good karate athlete has always been willing to work a little harder and perhaps a little more often than the others! That is his biggest secret!

Blocking Techniques

KARATE DEFENSE begins with strong blocking techniques. Use your hands and arms to strike or block off the kicks and blows of your attacking opponent. Use your blocking hand on the same side as that of your forward foot. That is, if your left foot is in front, then use your left hand or arm to block. At the same time your upper body should be turned at about a 45-degree angle to give a smaller target to your attacker. Turn or twist your hip sharply as you "focus" your block. If you were to use the opposite hand to block, both the block and body balance would be a lot weaker!

Illus. 23

The Low Block

Illus. 23—This block is very good against kicks and punches to the stomach or the groin area. It can be used from either the forward or horse stance.

Illus. 24—To practice the low block, stand in natural or ready stance and bring your right fist across your chest up to your opposite ear. The palm of your hand should be facing your ear at the start. Keep your left arm in front of your body with your fist about 8 inches away from your thigh.

Bring your right hand downwards across your chest, while pulling your left hand back straight to your hip in a sharp twisting motion (Illus. 25). Focus your block strongly about 8 inches in front of your right thigh. The outer edge of your wrist or your fist becomes the blocking area.

Illus. 24   Illus. 25

Illus. 26

The Outside Forearm Block

Illus. 26—Sometimes called the middle block, the outside forearm block protects your chest and stomach area. The outer edge of your forearm is used to block the opponent's blow—the block being made from the outside position of your body towards the inside and stopping about the middle of your body. This block is often used from both the forward and horse stance.

Illus. 27—Start by raising your right fist up next to your ear, with your knuckles facing front. Hold your left hand out straight in front of your body.

Illus. 28—Bring your right fist forward sharply now in a circular movement, at a slight downward angle. At the last instant, twist your right forearm quickly so that the palm of your fist is facing you. Pull your left hand back to your hip strongly, to add power to the block (see Illus. 26).

Illus. 27   Illus. 28

Illus. 29

The High Block

Illus. 29—Your face and neck areas can be most easily protected with the high block. Block your opponent's blow by an upward twisting motion of your blocking arm. Most *karatekas* prefer the forward stance when using this block.

Illus. 30—To practice the high block, take the natural stance. Cock your right fist just above your hip, with your left hand held out straight in front of your body. The palm of your right fist should be facing upwards at this stage.

Illus. 30

Illus. 31

Illus. 31—Bring your right hand across your chest and upwards under your chin.

Illus. 32—Raise your blocking arm with an upward, twisting motion of your forearm. Focus the block strongly just above your head, while pulling your left hand back to your hip hard! The palm of your blocking hand should now be facing front.

Illus. 32

Illus. 33

The Knifehand Block

Illus. 33—The knifehand block usually follows from a back stance although it can be used as well from other stances. To form a correct knifehand, try to keep your four fingers pressed together. Bend your thumb and force it outward so that the heel of your palm remains flat. Do not bend your wrist. Use the outer edge of your knifehand as the blocking surface.

33

Start with your right hand held straight in front of your body. Raise your left hand to your opposite ear, with the palm of your knifehand facing the ear. (Illus. 34).

Illus. 34

Illus. 35

Bring your left hand across your chest now
(Illus. 35) to the opposite side of your body.

Illus. 36

Focus the block against your opponent's punch by moving your left arm in the direction of the punch. Twist your forearm hard as the blow arrives and tense your chest muscles while pulling your right hand back to your chest, palm upwards (Illus. 36 and 33).

The "X" Block

This is a good, fast block against all types of attacks to your face and neck. It requires very little strength (Illus. 37).

Illus. 37

Illus. 38   Illus. 39

Cross your hands in front of your chest (Illus. 38) with either open hands or closed fists. Keep your hands open if you intend to grab your opponent's arm after the block.

Illus. 39—Quickly raise your crossed hands above your forehead. Be sure to keep your elbows in line with your body. The block will be weak if your elbows are allowed to spread.

The Karate Fist

ILLUS. 40—Begin with your hand in "open" position.

Illus. 41—Next, roll your fingers into a ball, and press your thumb against your rolled-up index and middle fingers.

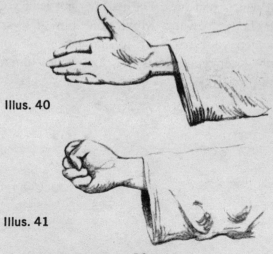

Illus. 40

Illus. 41

THE STRAIGHT KARATE PUNCH

While the uppercut and hooking motions are often used in karate punches, you will depend mostly on a straight speedy lunge punch and a powerful reverse punch.

In the lunge punch, your striking fist is on the same side as your advancing foot, while the reverse punch is thrown from the same side as your rear leg. The lunge punch is made as your front leg touches the ground, using the forward movement of your entire body along with thrust of your rear leg. More power is possible in the reverse punch because of the rotating thrust of your hip as the punch is delivered.

Remember the basic principles of body movement which you have learned. Do not lean your upper body forward. Move your hips first and straighten your back leg to add power to your punch. Keep your heels flat, and your stomach thrust forward.

Illus. 42

Illus. 42—In the straight karate punch, strike the target with the first two knuckles of the fist.

How to Practice the Straight Punch

Illus. 43—For best results, as a student, you should not attempt punching practice while moving until you are punching reasonably well from the standing position. You do not want to land a punch, just show that you can.

Illus. 43

Illus. 44

Illus. 45

Illus. 44—Start from the natural or ready stance. Extend your left hand in front of your body, palm down. Place your right fist just above your hip with the palm of your fist facing upwards.

The punch must reach its target in a straight line—like an arrow shot from a bow. Turn your right forearm with a twisting motion just as your elbow passes upward above your stomach. Your open left hand should be pulled halfway back to your hip at this point (Illus. 45).

As you punch straight ahead at shoulder height, the palm of your fist faces downward. Raising your right arm, twisting it, and punching forward should be all one lightning-fast motion. Your left hand stays at your hip, palm upwards, ready for the next move (Illus. 46). On all straight punches, your arm should rub the side of your body as the punch leaves your hip.

Illus. 46

THE REVERSE PUNCH

Known as karate's strongest punch, the reverse punch is mainly used in counterattack, after you have blocked your opponent's punch or kick. A twisting thrust of the hip thrown into the forward movement of the body adds to the power of the attack (Illus. 47).

Illus. 47

Start from a low forward stance. Extend your left hand out to the front, and pull back your right fist just above your hip. Keep your hip at a 45-degree angle (Illus. 48).

Illus. 48

Illus. 49

Draw your left hand back as your right fist shoots out in a straight line (Illus. 49).

Illus. 50

Push back hard on your rear foot as you twist your hip forward! Your body should be facing directly front at the end of the punch (Illus. 50).

THE BACK FIST

Turn your fist so that the closed palm faces back towards you, and use the first two knuckles as the striking surface in this speedy technique.

Although used mainly against soft targets, like the face and stomach, the back fist has proven to be a very good surprise weapon! The force of the blow does not travel in a straight line, as in a straight punch, but more in a half circle. It can be aimed at the front, side or rear.

The motion is a fast snapping of the forearm and elbow. Because of this, it is important to keep your elbow slightly bent at the end of the strike to avoid injury to your elbow joint (Illus. 51).

Illus. 51

Illus. 52

Illus. 52—To practice the back fist strike, start by crossing both arms in front of your body with your striking fist on top.

Illus. 53—Deliver the strike quickly in a half-circular motion. The punch is simply a snapping movement of your forearm and elbow. At the end of the strike, the bottom part of your fist may be facing either downwards or sideways, depending on how the target was struck.

Illus. 53

THE FIST HAMMER

Here you use the fleshy bottom part of your fist (not your wristbone) to strike the target very much as if you were using a hammer (Illus. 54).

Illus. 54

Illus. 55

The targets are the bony parts of the body like the shoulder blades and ribs. The blow may be directed downwards or sideways.

As with the back fist strike, this blow depends on the fast snapping action of your forearm and elbow, as well as the tensing of your shoulder muscles.

Illus. 55—As in the back fist strike, cross both arms in front of your body, and bring your strik-

53

Illus. 56

ing fist upwards in a half circle to the side. At the very start of this movement, twist your wrist with a snapping motion so that the bottom part of your fist is facing upwards.

Illus. 56—Continue the half-circle movement so that the bottom part of your fist now faces downwards as it strikes the target!

54

Strikes

The Palm Heel Strike

ILLUS. 57—Use caution in practicing this technique to avoid injury to your partner.

Illus. 57

Here you use the heel of your palm very much like a straight punch to your opponent's face at an upward angle! This blow can be delivered upwards at his jaw or sideways to his ribs. It is also often used as a block against punching and kicking attacks.

Illus. 58

Start by standing in natural or ready stance, with your left palm extended in front of your body, and your right fist just above your hip (Illus. 58).

Illus. 59—Open your right fist and thrust your hand forward. Turn your right wrist so that your

Illus. 59

fingers are pointing upwards. At the same time pull back your left hand sharply to your hip.

Illus. 60—Shoot out your palm heel in a straight line upwards, but like a punch. Your left hand should now be cocked just above your left hip, ready for the next move.

Illus. 60

Elbow Strikes

Your elbow may be employed to attack targets at the front, side or rear. You can use it in an upwards, sidewards or downwards direction. Powerful and very good for close infighting, the elbow strike is easy to learn. For this reason it is preferred by many who specialize in self-defense techniques.

Sideward Elbow Strike

Illus. 61—The sideward elbow strike works best when applied from the horse stance. This technique would be weak if used from the back stance, because it does not allow a strong enough balance to the sides.

Illus. 61

Illus. 62

Illus. 62—Stand in natural stance and cross
your arms in front of your body.

Illus. 63

Illus. 63—Thrust outwards towards the target, keeping your striking elbow in a straight line.

Downward Elbow Strike

Illus. 64—The targets for the downward strike are the neck or upper back, or, if the opponent is flat on his back, the chest. The forward stance is preferred for this technique.

Illus. 64

Illus. 65   Illus. 66

Illus. 65—Starting, raise your fist straight overhead.

Illus. 66—Thrust your elbow downward sharply to the target. Your elbow should be about 6 inches away from your body, not alongside it.

The Sideward Knifehand Strike

Illus. 67—This open-hand blow gets its power from the sharp, snapping motion of your elbow and wrist. The targets are your opponent's temple and neck, and you strike with the outer edge of your hand.

Illus. 67

Illus. 68—Bring up your striking hand to your ear. Do not raise your shoulder. Raising the shoulder prevents proper tensing of the chest muscles during the strike. To form a knifehand, flatten the heel of your palm by bending your thumb outward.

Illus. 69—Swing your knifehand in a sweeping arc very much like using a whip. Your palm should be facing up and your wrist bent at the end of the strike.

Illus. 68   Illus. 69

Kicks

The Front Snap Kick

THIS SPEEDY kick is delivered from the forward stance with your rear foot. Your front foot—Illus. 70—can be used to kick from the back

Illus. 70

stance, but the kick is somewhat weaker since it does not have the forward thrust of your body behind it.

The snapping action of your knee and the forward thrust of your body should be combined in one smooth motion. Only the ball of your foot should be used as the striking surface. Keep the toes of your kicking foot curled upwards to avoid injury to them (Illus. 72). Almost any part of your opponent's body, such as the head, chest and stomach can be attacked with the front kick.

After the kick, your foot must be pulled back quickly to keep your opponent from grabbing it.

For basic front-kick practice, stand with your feet together, both knees slightly bent. The important thing is to remember that your kicking foot starts by being raised just above the knee level of the supporting leg (Illus. 71).

Illus. 72—Quickly bring up your kicking leg with the snapping action of your knee, to execute the kick. Pull your kicking foot back to knee level just as fast as you can. Then slowly lower your leg to the floor.

Illus. 71

Illus. 72

The Side Thrust Kick

Either the edge of your foot or your heel may be used as the striking surface with the side thrust kick. The striking power of the kick comes from the thrust of the hip into the kick (Illus. 73).

The side thrust kick gives you a longer reach and greater power than is possible with other

Illus. 73

Illus. 74

kicks. It is very good against hard targets like
the knees, ribs and chin.

When practicing the kick, start from the natural stance. Bring your kicking foot up to the
knee of your supporting leg (Illus. 74). If you
want to execute a high side kick, then you must
raise your knee even higher.

71

Illus. 75

Push your kicking leg straight out to the side. Thrust your hip strongly into the kick for power. Lean your upper body towards the direction of the kick (Illus. 75). If you lean away from the kick, both your kick and body balance will be weak. Keep your left fist tight at your side.

Illus. 76—Quickly return your kicking foot to the knee level of the supporting leg, and gently lower your foot to the floor.

Illus. 76

The Side Snap Kick

Illus. 77—The snapping action of the knee of your kicking foot is used in the side snap kick for its quick striking power. Soft places such as the opponent's groin, throat and face are the targets of the outer edge of the kicking foot.

Your kicking leg is never extended all the way, as in the thrust kick. Pull back your kicking leg a split second before your knee swings out straight, to avoid injury to your knee joint.

Illus. 77

Illus. 78

Start by standing in the natural stance. Quickly raise your kicking foot up to the knee height of your supporting leg (Illus. 78).

75

Illus. 79

Illus. 79—Complete the kick to the side by using the snapping action of your knee. Pull back your kicking leg just before it is fully extended.

76

The Roundhouse Kick

Both the rotating movement of your body and the snapping knee action of your kicking foot are used in the roundhouse kick (Illus. 80). Like the roundhouse punch, the kick travels in a sideways half-circle movement. The ball of your foot is the striking surface for such targets as your opponent's face, neck, stomach and ribs.

Illus. 80

Use either foot in practicing the roundhouse kick. Start from the natural stance or the right forward stance. Bring up your bent right leg sideways (Illus. 81). At the same time, start to move your right arm to your rear.

Illus. 81

Illus. 82

Illus. 82—Pivot halfway round on the ball of your left foot while rotating your entire body forward. Add the snapping action of your knee just before your foot hits the target. Your upper body should be in a half-front-facing position to the target. If your body is rotated too far, your balance will be weakened, and it will be difficult to defend yourself against a counterattack if your roundhouse kick fails. After the kick is completed, draw your foot back to the starting position.

The Back Kick

The back kick is most useful against an opponent who is attacking you from behind. Thrust the heel of your foot straight back at a slight upward angle (Illus. 83). Your opponent's stomach, chest and groin are the main target areas.

Illus. 83

Illus. 84

Illus. 84—Starting from the natural stance, cock your kicking foot by bringing it up to the knee level of your supporting leg, which you keep slightly bent. Look over your shoulder, on the kicking-leg side, at your target.

81

Illus. 85

Thrust your kicking leg in a straight line at your target (Illus. 85). Draw your kicking foot back to knee level before lowering it to the floor.

The Stamping Heel Kick

This is simply a defensive move against the grabbing attacks from the rear. It is very effective and not difficult to learn. Thrust the heel of your kicking foot down hard on your attacker's shin or instep (Illus. 86).

Illus. 86

Illus. 87

Stand in the natural stance to start and raise your kicking foot to knee level. Look down on your kicking side at the target (Illus. 87).

Drive your heel down strongly to the floor. Practice stopping your heel barely an inch off the floor, to develop speed and control (Illus. 88). Withdraw your kicking foot quickly to knee level and return it to starting position.

Illus. 88

The Spinning Wheel Kick

Sometimes called the hook kick, the spinning wheel kick is like a roundhouse kick but done in reverse. It uses the turning movement of your rotating body and the backward snapping knee action of your kicking leg for its striking power.

The back of your heel serves as the striking or hooking surface (Illus. 89). It is very important to remember that your entire body must pivot on

Illus. 89

Illus. 90

the ball of your supporting foot to cut down
strain on your supporting leg.

The wheel kick can be performed from the
front or off to the side of your opponent. If you
are facing your opponent with your left leg forward, move your left foot directly across, about
12 inches past the toes of your right leg (Illus.
90). Be sure to place your body weight directly
on the ball of your *left* foot.

Illus. 91

Illus. 91—Whip your *right* leg up sideways as you pivot and rotate your chest backwards. At the same time, turn your head in the same direction. Your entire body must spin quickly, in a tight circle, as you spin on the ball of your left foot.

Illus. 92—Continue your spinning movement and focus on your target with the back of your heel. Swing your right hand around, as in the back-fist strike, to protect your exposed back during the kick.

Illus. 92

Contests

BASIC SEMI-FREE SPARRING

LONG BEFORE you master all the basic kicks and blows, you have to practice a very important training exercise called semi-free sparring. This is a series of attack and defense moves, decided upon beforehand, which helps to train and sharpen your reflexes.

One-Step Semi-Free Sparring

Two opponents face each other in the "ready" stance, an arm's length apart. One plays the part of the attacker, while the other defends against the attack that he knows is coming.

For example—let us decide that the attack will be a straight punch to the face. The attacker drops smartly into a forward stance in a regular low block position, with one hand held above the thigh and the other fist cocked at the hip. The

Illus. 93

defender remains in the "ready" stance, awaiting the attack (Illus. 93).

The attacking student must go forward one full step in making the attack. At the same time the defender drops back a step, blocks the expected punch, and counterattacks. In this case, he steps back into a forward stance, using a high block, and counters with a reverse punch to the face or body.

Always exhale sharply and yell or shout while counterattacking! This yell or shout is called *kiai* in karate. *Kiai* helps to tense your body muscles and focus the most power for that split second just as your blow reaches the target!

Use full power in your kicks and punches, but stop them just short of touching your partner to prevent injury.

After the one-step, you can go on to three-step and five-step semi-free sparring exercises. The only difference is that the attack is carried forward three and five steps, with the defender counterattacking only on the last block. You always decide in advance what the moves will be.

Semi-free sparring may be practiced by two *karatekas* by themselves or in a group with the instructor giving the commands.

FREE-STYLE SPARRING

The main purpose of karate training is to enable you to use karate techniques you have learned in the early pages of this book in what is called free-style sparring. This is the closest thing to real combat, where none of the moves are decided on beforehand. Each contestant is free to use the techniques he prefers.

A match between two opponents is held under strict contest rules. Any action that might harm your opponent is forbidden. The kicks and blows are strongly "focused," but never touch the opponent.

It is the duty of the referee to start and stop the match and to enforce the rules (Illus. 94). Good sportsmanship and the proper respect for your opponent and the contest official must be

Illus. 94

Illus. 95

observed. Losing your temper, recklessly using dangerous techniques, or purposely hitting your opponent, are grounds for immediate disqualification! The easiest way to lose a match is by losing your temper!

To score a point, the techniques must be cleanly performed and strongly focused. How

94

well you do in free-style sparring depends very much on how seriously you have practiced your basic techniques and on the training you have had in basic semi-free sparring. There is no time to think in free-style fighting. Your trained reflexes must react instantly against a sudden, unexpected attack! The experienced *karateka* never stops practicing his basic techniques.

Illus. 95—The referee rushes in to stop the action as a *karateka* scores a point with a leaping, punching attack!

Illus. 96—Point scored! A hard punching attack is stopped by a well-executed wheel kick to the ribs!

Illus. 96

Katas

TO AN average person, the karate *katas* or forms look almost like a dance routine. Actually they are a training drill. The moves in each *kata* are decided beforehand and performed one after the other until the *kata* is finished. These moves represent the techniques of defense and counterattack which you would use when forced to fight

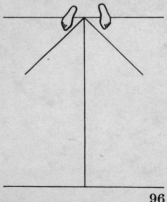

Illus. 97

two, three, or even five, opponents at the same time. To perform the *katas* properly, you must first have a fair amount of skill in the basic karate techniques. The *kata* expert makes the *kata* come alive with a combination of grace, speed and power!

Some *katas* are slow, but most combine both fast and slow movements. Presented here for the young *karateka* is *kata* No. 1, which is used in most Japanese and Korean styles and in some of the newer American styles of karate.

Form or Kata #1 (Heian Shodan)

Illus. 98—Stand in ready stance. Bow from the waist.

Illus. 99—Turn your head quickly to your left as if you were expecting an attack from that direction. Pivot on your right foot to your left side as you execute a low block from the left forward stance.

Illus. 100—Step forward with your right foot, and deliver a lunge punch with your right hand from the right forward stance.

Illus. 101—Pivot on your left foot to your right side, and turn around 180 degrees (a half circle) to your opposite rear. At the same time execute a low block from the right forward stance.

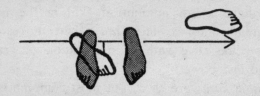

Illus. 98   Illus. 99

Illus. 100

Illus. 101

Illus. 102—Pull back your right arm in a wide circular motion as you draw your right foot back within 10 inches of your left leg.

Illus. 102

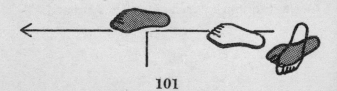

Illus. 103

Illus. 104

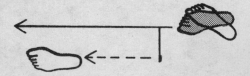

Illus. 103—Continue the circular motion of your right hand, and focus a strong fist hammer blow at shoulder level.

Illus. 104—Move forward into the left forward stance, and lunge punch with your left hand.

Illus. 105   Illus. 106

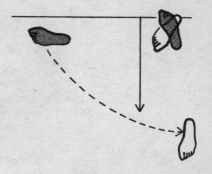

Illus. 105—Look to your left. Before moving, always glance quickly in the direction of the turn that you intend to make.

Illus. 106—Turn on your right foot 90 degrees (a quarter circle) to your left into the left forward stance while doing a low block.

Illus. 107

Illus. 107—Without moving from the position in Illus. 106, immediately do a high block with open hand.

104

Illus. 108—Step forward with your right foot into a right forward stance. Use a right high block with fist closed.

Illus. 108

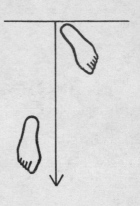

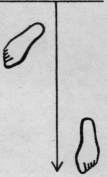

Illus. 109

Illus. 109—Move into left forward stance—left high block.

Illus. 110

Illus. 110—Step forward—right forward stance
—right high block.

Illus. 111

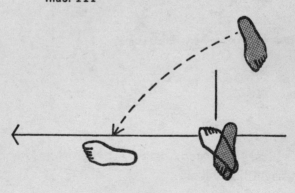

Illus. 111—Pivot towards your rear and turn 270 degrees (three-quarters of a circle) while executing a left low block from the left forward

stance. Beginners sometimes find this move difficult. Turn on your right foot completely to your
rear and keep on turning 90 degrees (a quarter
circle) more to your left.

Illus. 112—Step forward with your right foot
into the right forward stance—and make a right
lunge punch.

Illus. 112

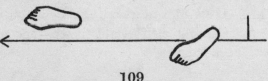

Illus. 113

Illus. 114

Illus. 113—Pivot on your rear foot towards your right, making a 180-degree turn (half circle) to your rear. Execute a right low block from the right forward stance.

Illus. 114—Move forward one step with your left foot—into a left forward stance—and make a left lunge punch.

Illus. 115—Turn 90 degrees (one-quarter turn) to your left on your rear foot into a left forward stance—make a left low block.

Illus. 115

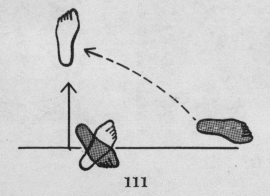

111

Illus. 115, 116, 117 and 118 are all shown facing front, but in the actual *kata* pattern, you would be moving forward with your back towards the camera. But to better show the movement, these four progressive steps have been shown from the front position.

Illus. 116—Move forward one step—into a right forward stance—and make a right lunge punch.

Illus. 117—Step into a left forward stance—and make a left lunge punch.

Illus. 116   Illus. 117

Illus. 118

Illus. 118—Move your right foot forward into a right forward stance—make a lunge punch, and yell: *kiai*.

Illus. 119—As in Illus. 111, pivot on your right foot to your rear and move to your left until you complete a 270-degree (three-quarters) turn. As you turn, drop into a left back stance and execute a left knifehand block.

Illus. 119

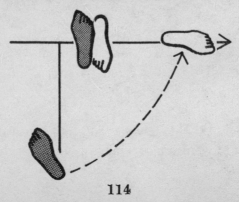

Illus. 120—Step forward, with your right foot at a 45-degree angle, into a right back stance with a right knifehand block.

Illus. 120

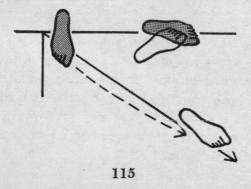

Illus. 121

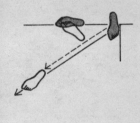

Illus. 122

Illus. 121—Pivot on your rear foot to your right—until you are facing exactly opposite from the position in Illus. 119. Execute a knifehand block with your right hand from a back stance.

Illus. 122—Move your left foot forward at a 45-degree angle into a back stance while executing a left knifehand block.

Illus. 123—Withdraw your left foot back to a ready stance. Bow from the waist.

End of *Kata* #1.

Illus. 123

Karate Ranks

DIFFERENT COLORED belts are worn by karate students to show the rank or grade that they have earned. Most karate systems or styles use white uniforms, while some other styles prefer black uniforms. Karate is so widely practiced throughout the world, differences in the color of belts and uniforms do exist. Most Korean, Okinawan and Japanese styles employ a white jacket and trousers. A beginner starts with a white belt. After that come yellow, green, purple, brown and finally the black belt.

All grades below black belt are called student grades. They are referred to as *Kup* in Korean and *Kyu* in Japanese. When a student first joins a karate class, he wears a white belt which stands for grade 9. He then goes on to grades 8 and 7, both yellow belts. Grades 6 and 5 are green and grade 4 is purple. Grades 3, 2 and 1 are brown. When you reach the rank of brown belt 1, you have earned your right to try for a black belt.

Index